Scaling Climate Finance: A Global Climate Solutions Insight on Green Bonds, Carbon Markets, and Investment Pathways for a Net-Zero Future

1

Copyright

Scaling Climate Finance: A Global Climate Solutions Insight on Green Bonds, Carbon Markets, and Investment Pathways for a Net-Zero Future

ISBNs:

• eBook: **978-1-991369-23-9**

• Paperback: **978-1-991369-24-6**

Disclaimer

This publication is intended for informational purposes only. While every effort has been made to ensure the accuracy and reliability of the information contained herein, the author and publisher make no representations or warranties, express or implied, regarding the completeness, accuracy, or applicability of the content. Any reliance on the information provided in this book is at the reader's own discretion. The author and publisher shall not be liable for any loss or damage arising directly or indirectly from the use of this publication.

The opinions expressed in this book are those of the author and do not necessarily reflect the views of any affiliated organizations, institutions, or individuals. Readers are encouraged to seek professional advice before making financial, policy, or investment decisions based on the material presented.

Author and Publisher Rights:

The author and publisher reserve the right to revise, update, or remove any content in this book at their sole discretion, without prior notice.

Printed and distributed worldwide.

Table of Contents

Executive Summary

The transition to a low-carbon economy requires a scalable, transparent, and efficient climate finance system. Green bonds and carbon markets play a critical role in mobilizing capital for climate mitigation, adaptation, and sustainable development projects. As global investment needs exceed $100 trillion, expanding these financial instruments is essential to achieving net-zero targets and advancing the Sustainable Development Goals (SDGs).

Green bonds have emerged as a mainstream financing tool, funding renewable energy, sustainable infrastructure, and biodiversity conservation. Despite rapid growth, challenges such as greenwashing, regulatory fragmentation, and lack of harmonized taxonomies must be addressed to enhance market credibility and investor confidence. Strengthening reporting frameworks and policy incentives will be key to unlocking their full potential.

Carbon markets provide a market-driven solution to emissions reductions, using cap-and-trade systems, carbon taxes, and offset trading to internalize the cost of carbon pollution. Ensuring market integrity, additionality, and transparency is critical, particularly under the Paris Agreement's Article 6 framework. Robust oversight and standardization will reinforce confidence and prevent market distortions.

Policymakers, investors, and financial institutions must work together to expand sovereign green bonds, strengthen carbon pricing mechanisms, and integrate climate risk into financial regulations. By aligning public and private sector investments, scaling green finance can accelerate the transition to a resilient, net-zero global economy while fostering long-term financial stability.

Introduction

The global climate finance landscape has expanded significantly in recent years, driven by the increasing urgency to address climate change and transition to a low-carbon economy. Governments, financial institutions, and businesses are recognizing the necessity of mobilizing capital at scale to fund mitigation and adaptation initiatives. However, despite the progress made, there remains a substantial gap between current investment levels and the estimated $100 trillion+ needed to achieve global decarbonization targets. Meeting this challenge requires innovative financial mechanisms that can attract institutional investors, enhance market credibility, and ensure effective capital deployment toward sustainable projects.

Green bonds and carbon markets have emerged as two of the most promising instruments for scaling climate finance. Green bonds provide a structured means of raising capital for environmentally beneficial projects, offering transparency and accountability through established reporting frameworks. Meanwhile, carbon markets create economic incentives for emissions reduction, using mechanisms such as emissions trading systems (ETS) and voluntary carbon markets (VCM) to drive investments in low-carbon technologies and sustainable practices. When effectively designed and implemented, these instruments can play a crucial role in bridging the climate finance gap, supporting both public and private sector commitments to net-zero goals.

This Insight explores the opportunities, challenges, and policy reforms necessary to expand the role of green bonds and carbon markets in global climate finance. It provides a policy-driven analysis of how these mechanisms can be scaled to accelerate investment in climate action while ensuring market integrity, investor confidence, and long-term financial sustainability.

Chapter 1: Green Bonds: Mobilizing Capital for Sustainable Investments

Green bonds have become a vital financial instrument for directing capital toward sustainable projects that support climate action and environmental sustainability. As fixed-income securities specifically earmarked for green investments, they provide investors with a structured way to contribute to the low-carbon transition while generating returns. Over the past decade, the green bond market has grown rapidly, attracting sovereign issuers, municipalities, corporations, and financial institutions seeking to align their investments with environmental objectives.

Defining Green Bonds and Their Role in Climate Finance

Green bonds have become a key financial instrument in global efforts to combat climate change and promote sustainability. These bonds function similarly to traditional fixed-income securities but are issued specifically to finance projects with clear environmental benefits. Over the past decade, the green bond market has grown rapidly, driven by investor demand for sustainable finance and regulatory support for climate-related investments.

Green Bonds as a Fixed-Income Instrument for Environmental Projects

A green bond is a fixed-income security issued by governments, corporations, financial institutions, or multilateral organizations to raise capital for environmentally sustainable projects. Like conventional bonds, they provide investors with regular interest payments and the return of principal at maturity. However, their key distinction is that proceeds must be allocated exclusively to projects that generate measurable environmental benefits.

Eligible green bond projects include:

• **Renewable energy** (solar, wind, hydro, geothermal).

• **Energy efficiency** (green buildings, smart grids).

• **Sustainable water management** (wastewater treatment, flood protection).

• **Pollution prevention** (waste management, air quality improvements).

• **Biodiversity conservation** (reforestation, marine protection).

• **Sustainable transportation** (electric vehicles, public transit).

To ensure transparency and accountability, green bond issuers follow recognized frameworks such as:

• **ICMA Green Bond Principles (GBP)**: Voluntary guidelines covering use of proceeds, project evaluation, fund management, and reporting.

• **Climate Bonds Initiative (CBI) Certification**: A global standard verifying that bonds meet strict environmental criteria.

These frameworks provide investors with assurance that funds are allocated toward legitimate climate and sustainability projects.

Differences Between Green Bonds and Other Sustainable Debt Instruments

Green bonds belong to a broader category of sustainable finance instruments, including blue bonds, social bonds, and sustainability-linked bonds (SLBs). Each serves distinct environmental, social, or governance (ESG) goals.

1. Blue Bonds

A subset of green bonds, blue bonds finance ocean and marine sustainability projects, supporting:

• Sustainable fisheries and marine conservation.

• Coastal resilience projects to protect against rising sea levels.

• Ocean pollution reduction, such as plastic waste management.

The Republic of Seychelles issued the first sovereign blue bond in 2018, funding sustainable marine development. Since then, blue bonds have gained traction among island nations and coastal economies.

2. Social Bonds

Social bonds finance projects with direct social impact, rather than purely environmental benefits. These include:

• Affordable housing and clean water access.

• Healthcare, education, and job creation programs.

• Pandemic response and economic recovery efforts.

During the COVID-19 pandemic, social bonds were widely issued to support healthcare and economic relief. Like green bonds, social bonds require strict reporting to ensure funds are used for their intended purpose.

3. SLBs

SLBs differ from green and social bonds in that they are not tied to specific projects. Instead, they are linked to an issuer's overall sustainability performance.

Key features:

• Companies commit to long-term ESG targets, such as reducing carbon emissions.

• Interest rates adjust based on whether targets are met (penalties apply if missed).

• Greater flexibility than green bonds, as funds are not restricted to specific projects.

SLBs align corporate financial strategy with climate goals, offering an alternative to traditional green bonds while promoting net-zero commitments.

Growth of the Green Bond Market

The green bond market has evolved from a niche financial instrument to a mainstream mechanism for financing sustainability. Investor demand for ESG investments and increasing regulatory support have made green bonds a key tool for funding climate mitigation, adaptation, and resilience projects. The growth of clear taxonomies, reporting frameworks, and policy incentives has further strengthened their role in mobilizing capital for sustainability.

Historical Evolution and Growth of Green Bonds

The green bond market originated in 2007 with the European Investment Bank's (EIB) Climate Awareness Bond, followed by the World Bank's first green bond in 2008. These early issuances established fixed-income securities as a viable tool for financing environmental projects.

Key milestones in green bond market development:

• **2013**: The first corporate green bond was issued by EDF, a French energy company, demonstrating private sector participation.

• **2014**: The International Capital Market Association (ICMA) introduced the GBP, providing voluntary guidelines for issuers.

• **2017**: Green bond issuance exceeded $100 billion annually, transitioning into a mainstream investment class.

• **2020**: The total green bond market surpassed $1 trillion in cumulative issuance, showing resilience despite the COVID-19 pandemic.

• **2023**: Total issuance exceeded $3 trillion, expanding into emerging markets and new sectors like sustainable agriculture and blue economy projects.

This exponential growth reflects the increasing integration of sustainability into financial markets, positioning green bonds as a key instrument in climate finance.

Key Players in the Green Bond Market

Green bond issuance spans multiple sectors and regions, with participation from governments, financial institutions, corporations, and development banks.

• **Sovereign Governments**: National governments issue sovereign green bonds to finance public-sector sustainability projects like renewable energy and low-carbon transport. Leading issuers include France, Germany, China, and the UK.

• **Municipal and Local Governments**: Cities such as New York, San Francisco, and London finance climate resilience projects through green bonds.

• **Financial Institutions**: Banks like HSBC, BNP Paribas, and Goldman Sachs structure, underwrite, and invest in green bonds.

• **Corporations**: Companies in energy, utilities, manufacturing, and technology issue green bonds to fund climate-friendly projects and supply chain decarbonization.

• **Multilateral Development Banks (MDBs)**: Institutions like the World Bank, EIB, and Asian Development Bank (ADB) are among the largest issuers, supporting sustainability projects worldwide.

Importance of Taxonomies and Reporting Frameworks

As the green bond market expands, ensuring credibility and transparency is essential. Investors need clear definitions and reliable reporting to confirm that proceeds fund legitimate climate projects. Several frameworks have been developed to provide standardized guidelines.

1. EU Green Bond Standard (EUGBS)

The EU Green Bond Standard creates a uniform regulatory framework to enhance market integrity. Key features:

• Strict eligibility criteria, ensuring alignment with the EU Taxonomy for Sustainable Activities.

• Mandatory third-party verification of green bond projects.

• Detailed impact reporting to enhance transparency and investor confidence.

The EUGBS serves as a global benchmark, influencing green bond standards worldwide.

2. ICMA GBP

The ICMA Green Bond Principles provide voluntary best practices for issuers, covering:

• **Use of proceeds**: Funds must be allocated to environmentally beneficial projects.

• **Project evaluation**: Issuers must disclose eligibility criteria.

• **Fund management**: Proceeds should be tracked separately.

• **Impact reporting**: Issuers should provide annual updates on project outcomes.

The GBP has been widely adopted across governments, corporations, and financial institutions, reinforcing market credibility.

3. CBI Certification

The CBI Certification Scheme applies science-based criteria to ensure green bond eligibility aligns with Paris Agreement targets. Many issuers seek third-party verification through this certification to enhance investor confidence.

Challenges and Policy Considerations for Scaling Green Bonds

Green bonds have become a major tool for financing sustainable projects, yet several challenges remain in ensuring their credibility, transparency, and accessibility. As the market grows, policymakers, investors, and issuers must address key concerns related to transparency, additionality, greenwashing, and the need for harmonized standards. Additionally, governments and financial institutions play a crucial role in expanding green bond accessibility through incentives, public-private partnerships (PPPs), and credit enhancement mechanisms. Addressing these challenges will be essential for scaling green bond markets and ensuring their effectiveness in financing climate action.

Ensuring Transparency, Additionality, and Credibility in Green Bond Markets

For green bonds to function as a trusted financial instrument, they must adhere to high transparency standards, ensuring that proceeds are allocated to legitimate climate-positive projects. Key concerns include:

• **Transparency in Fund Allocation**: Investors require clear reporting on how green bond proceeds are used to verify that funds support environmentally beneficial projects. Without transparency, the risk of misallocation increases, reducing investor confidence.

• **Additionality of Green Bond Projects**: Additionality refers to ensuring that green bond-funded projects would not have been financed without the bond issuance. Some critics argue that green bonds often finance projects that would have proceeded anyway, reducing their true environmental impact. To address this, issuers must demonstrate that their projects go beyond business-as-usual investments.

• **Impact Measurement and Reporting**: Issuers must provide regular impact reports detailing how green bond proceeds are used and what environmental benefits they generate. Adhering to frameworks such as the ICMA Green Bond Principles and CBI Certification helps standardize these reporting practices.

By strengthening transparency, additionality, and impact reporting, green bond markets can enhance investor confidence and attract more capital to sustainable finance.

Addressing Concerns of Greenwashing and the Need for Harmonized Standards

A growing concern in the green bond market is greenwashing, where issuers misrepresent their bonds as environmentally beneficial without clear accountability. Inconsistent definitions of "green" across jurisdictions increase the risk of greenwashing, making it difficult for investors to assess the credibility of green bonds.

• **Greenwashing Risks**: Some issuers label their bonds as "green" without clear alignment to scientific climate targets. This erodes trust in green finance and reduces market efficiency.

• **Need for Harmonized Taxonomies**: Different countries and financial institutions use varying definitions of green projects, creating inconsistencies in green bond evaluation. The EUGBS and China's Green Bond Endorsed Project Catalogue are examples of regional efforts to create structured taxonomies, but a globally harmonized framework is needed.

• **Mandatory Green Bond Verification**: Independent third-party verification and certification can help ensure that green bonds meet rigorous environmental and financial standards. Expanding the use of CBI certification and ICMA-aligned external reviews can mitigate greenwashing risks.

Developing a standardized global green finance framework will provide greater clarity, credibility, and comparability for investors, ultimately scaling green bond markets.

Role of Government Incentives, PPPs, and Credit Enhancement Mechanisms in Expanding Accessibility

While green bonds have gained popularity among large corporations and governments, smaller issuers and developing countries often face barriers to accessing green bond markets due to high issuance costs, lack of technical expertise, and perceived investment risks. Governments and financial institutions can expand accessibility through:

1. Government Incentives for Green Bond Issuance

• **Tax Incentives and Subsidies**: Some countries provide tax exemptions or reductions on green bond interest payments to encourage investment.

• **Regulatory Support**: Central banks and financial regulators can offer **preferential capital treatment** for green bonds, reducing funding costs for issuers.

• **Sovereign Green Bonds**: Governments can **issue sovereign green bonds** to **set a benchmark** for corporate green bond issuances, increasing market confidence.

2. PPPs to De-Risk Investments

• **Blended Finance Models**: PPPs can combine public capital (from development banks) with private investment, reducing financial risks for institutional investors.

• **Government Co-Financing**: Some governments co-finance green bond projects, making private investment more attractive by sharing project risks.

• **Municipal Green Bonds**: Local governments can partner with private investors to finance urban sustainability initiatives such as green infrastructure, energy-efficient buildings, and climate adaptation projects.

3. Credit Enhancement Mechanisms to Attract Institutional Investors

• **Guarantees and First-Loss Capital**: Development banks and climate finance institutions can offer guarantees or first-loss capital to reduce the perceived risk of green bond investments.

• **Green Bond Insurance**: Some financial institutions provide green bond insurance, making green bonds a more secure investment option.

• **Securitization of Green Assets**: By bundling smaller green investments into larger, tradable financial products, securitization can increase green bond liquidity and attract institutional investors such as pension funds and asset managers.

Expanding these mechanisms will help lower barriers to entry, enabling more entities—particularly in developing countries and small-scale sustainable projects—to access green bond financing.

Chapter 2: Carbon Markets: Incentivizing Decarbonization Through Market Mechanisms

Carbon markets have emerged as a crucial policy tool for reducing greenhouse gas (GHG) emissions by assigning a financial cost to carbon pollution. By leveraging market-based mechanisms, these systems create economic incentives for businesses and industries to transition toward low-carbon operations. Carbon pricing instruments, including ETS, carbon taxes, and VCM, enable companies to internalize the environmental costs of their emissions while encouraging investments in cleaner technologies and sustainable practices.

As carbon markets continue to evolve, ensuring transparency, regulatory alignment, and market integrity remains critical to their effectiveness. However, challenges such as price volatility, carbon leakage, and concerns over credit credibility need to be addressed to maximize their impact. This chapter explores the structure and role of carbon markets, the economic rationale for carbon pricing, and key policy measures that can strengthen market credibility and drive large-scale decarbonization.

Overview of Carbon Markets and Their Mechanisms

Carbon markets serve as an essential policy tool for reducing GHG emissions by assigning a financial cost to carbon pollution. These markets incentivize businesses and industries to adopt cleaner technologies and sustainable practices, supporting the transition to a low-carbon global economy. Carbon pricing mechanisms—such as cap-and-trade systems, carbon taxes, and carbon offsets—enable cost-effective emissions reductions while promoting private-sector investment in sustainability.

There are two primary types of carbon markets: compliance carbon markets (Emissions Trading Systems: ETS) and VCM. Each functions under different regulatory frameworks but contributes to global decarbonization efforts.

Distinction Between Compliance Carbon Markets (ETS) and VCM

1. Compliance Carbon Markets (ETS)

Compliance carbon markets are government-regulated programs requiring businesses to reduce emissions or purchase allowances. The most common model is the cap-and-trade system, where governments set a limit on emissions, distribute allowances, and allow companies to trade excess permits.

Key features:

• Legally mandated participation for high-emission industries such as energy, manufacturing, and transportation.

• Encourages cost-effective emissions reductions through carbon trading.

• Examples include the EU Emissions Trading System (EU ETS), China's National Carbon Market, and California's Cap-and-Trade Program.

2. VCM

Voluntary carbon markets operate outside regulatory frameworks, allowing businesses and individuals to purchase carbon credits to offset emissions. These markets are driven by corporate sustainability commitments, ESG goals, and investor preferences.

Key features:

• Allow companies to invest in emissions-reduction projects, such as reforestation, renewable energy, and methane capture.

• Governed by certification bodies such as the Gold Standard and Verra's Verified Carbon Standard (VCS).

• Used by businesses to meet net-zero targets or enhance ESG performance.

While compliance markets are mandated by governments, voluntary markets enable corporate climate action by expanding private-sector investment in sustainability projects.

Key Carbon Pricing Mechanisms

Carbon markets operate under different pricing models, with the most widely used including:

1. Cap-and-Trade Systems (ETS)

• Governments set an emissions cap for a sector or region.

• Companies receive or purchase emission allowances and can trade surplus credits if they reduce emissions.

• The cap declines over time, increasing the cost of pollution and driving emissions reductions.

2. Carbon Taxes

• Governments impose a fixed price per ton of CO_2 emissions, creating a direct financial incentive for emissions reductions.

• Unlike cap-and-trade, carbon taxes do not set an emissions cap but instead influence corporate behavior through pricing mechanisms.

• Examples include Sweden, Canada, and Singapore, which have implemented carbon taxes as part of their climate policies.

3. Carbon Offsets

• Companies can offset emissions by investing in projects that remove or reduce CO_2, such as forestation, carbon capture, and methane reduction.

• Widely used in voluntary carbon markets and some compliance markets.

4. Carbon Credit Trading

• Businesses can buy and sell carbon credits, representing one ton of CO_2 removed or reduced.

• Used as a market-driven solution when internal reductions are not feasible.

Major Regional and International Carbon Markets

1. European Union Emissions Trading System (EU ETS)

• Established in 2005, it is the world's largest and most developed cap-and-trade system.

• Covers power generation, industrial sectors, and intra-European aviation.

• The Fit for 55 package aims to reduce free allowances and expand market coverage.

2. China's National Carbon Market

• Launched in 2021, it is the largest ETS by emissions coverage, initially targeting power sector emissions.

• The Chinese government actively manages allowances and pricing, with plans to expand to industrial and transport sectors.

3. California Cap-and-Trade Program

• In operation since 2013, covering power plants, fuel distributors, and industrial emitters.

• Linked with Quebec's carbon market, enabling cross-border emissions trading.

• Integrates carbon offset credits to support emissions reduction projects.

Carbon Pricing as a Tool for Climate Action

Carbon pricing is a key policy instrument for reducing GHG emissions, assigning a financial cost to carbon pollution to drive decarbonization efforts. By making carbon-intensive activities more expensive, these mechanisms encourage businesses and consumers to shift toward cleaner energy sources, low-carbon technologies, and energy efficiency improvements. When effectively designed, carbon pricing stimulates innovation, mobilizes climate finance, and supports economic sustainability. However, ensuring social equity and avoiding economic distortions is crucial for its successful implementation.

Internalizing Environmental Externalities

Carbon pricing operates on the principle that polluters should bear the full environmental cost of their emissions. Without it, businesses and individuals do not account for the climate-related damages they cause, leading to overconsumption of fossil fuels and unsustainable economic growth.

There are two primary approaches to carbon pricing:

1. **Carbon Taxes**: A fixed price per ton of CO_2 emissions, making fossil fuels more expensive while encouraging cleaner alternatives.

2. **ETS**: A cap-and-trade system where governments set an emissions limit, allowing companies to buy, sell, or trade allowances, ensuring cost-effective reductions.

Besides driving emissions reductions, carbon pricing generates government revenue, which can be reinvested in climate adaptation, infrastructure, or redistributed as carbon dividends to mitigate cost burdens.

Carbon Pricing and Clean Technology Investment

For carbon pricing to drive meaningful decarbonization, prices must be set at levels that influence investment and behavioral change. A low carbon price fails to incentivize businesses and consumers to transition to low-carbon alternatives.

• **Encouraging Renewable Energy and Efficiency**: Higher carbon prices make fossil fuels costlier, prompting investments in solar, wind, hydro, and energy-efficient systems.

• **Shaping Corporate Strategies**: Businesses facing high carbon costs adopt low-emission production methods, carbon capture, and electrification.

• **Changing Consumer Behavior**: Consumers adjust by reducing energy consumption, switching to electric vehicles (EVs), and adopting sustainable practices.

To meet Paris Agreement targets, carbon prices should reach $50–$100 per ton of CO_2 by 2030, with gradual increases over time.

Ensuring Social Equity and Avoiding Economic Distortions

While effective in reducing emissions, carbon pricing can disproportionately impact low-income households and carbon-intensive industries. Policymakers must adopt measures to prevent economic burdens and carbon leakage:

1. **Revenue Recycling and Carbon Dividends**

• Redistribute carbon tax revenues through rebates, tax cuts, or public programs.

• Direct dividends to households offset higher energy costs, protecting vulnerable populations.

2. **Support for Low-Income Communities and Affected Industries**

• Subsidies or tax relief prevent financial strain on low-income families.

• Worker retraining programs support fossil-fuel-dependent communities transitioning to clean energy.

3. **Border Carbon Adjustments (BCAs) to Prevent Carbon Leakage**

• Tariffs on imported goods based on their carbon footprint level the playing field.

• The EU's Carbon Border Adjustment Mechanism (CBAM) ensures fair competition for domestic industries under carbon pricing.

4. Gradual Implementation and Market Predictability

• Phased price increases allow businesses and consumers to adapt.

• Stable policy frameworks prevent volatility, ensuring long-term investment planning.

5. Complementary Climate Policies

• Stronger emissions regulations (e.g., fuel efficiency standards, renewable energy mandates).

• Subsidies for clean technology (e.g., tax credits for EVs, energy-efficient systems).

• Public investments in sustainable infrastructure, such as green buildings and climate-resilient transport systems.

Strengthening the Integrity of Carbon Markets

Carbon markets play a crucial role in global decarbonization efforts, providing economic incentives for emissions reductions. However, as these markets expand, ensuring transparency, credibility, and regulatory oversight is essential. Issues such as double counting, additionality concerns, and market manipulation can undermine trust in carbon markets and limit their effectiveness. Additionally, the international carbon trading framework under Article 6 of the Paris Agreement introduces new complexities. Strengthening market governance and standardizing regulations will be key to ensuring the long-term integrity of carbon markets.

Key Challenges: Double Counting, Additionality, and Market Manipulation

1. Double Counting

• Occurs when the same emissions reduction is claimed by multiple entities, such as a company and a country.

• A major risk in international carbon trading, where both host and buyer countries may count the same carbon credit toward their targets.

• To prevent this, carbon markets need robust tracking systems, unique credit identifiers, and transparent registries.

2. Additionality Concerns

• Additionality ensures that carbon credit-funded projects create emissions reductions beyond business-as-usual activities.

• If a project would have happened without carbon finance, the credit does not represent real climate benefits.

• Strict third-party verification and eligibility criteria are needed to confirm project legitimacy.

3. Market Manipulation Risks

• As carbon markets grow, traders and speculators can drive artificial price volatility, making emissions reduction planning unpredictable.

• While liquidity is necessary, excessive speculation shifts focus away from emissions reduction.

• Regulatory safeguards, such as real-time transaction monitoring and position limits, are needed to prevent market distortions.

The Role of Article 6 in International Carbon Trading

The Paris Agreement's Article 6 provides a framework for international cooperation on carbon markets, allowing cross-border trading of emissions reductions to meet climate commitments more efficiently.

1. Article 6.2: Bilateral Trading of Emissions Reductions

• Allows countries to transfer Internationally Transferred Mitigation Outcomes (ITMOs) to meet Nationally Determined Contributions (NDCs).

• Requires corresponding adjustments to prevent double counting.

• Encourages regional carbon market linkages, such as between the EU ETS and other trading systems.

2. Article 6.4: A Global Carbon Credit Mechanism

• Establishes a centralized UN-supervised carbon market for public and private entities.

• Builds on the Kyoto Protocol's Clean Development Mechanism (CDM) but introduces stronger safeguards to prevent low-quality credits and greenwashing.

• Requires strict third-party verification and transparency standards.

While Article 6 enhances international climate cooperation, challenges remain in standardized reporting, enforcement, and oversight.

Regulatory Reforms and Standardization to Enhance Market Credibility

To scale carbon markets effectively, stronger regulations and harmonized standards are needed. Key policy recommendations include:

1. Global Harmonization of Carbon Market Standards

• Current market fragmentation leads to inconsistencies in pricing, verification, and reporting.

• Aligning certification standards with Article 6, ICROA, and CORSIA can enhance clarity and investor confidence.

2. Transparency and Disclosure Requirements

• Publicly accessible emissions registries should track credit ownership to prevent fraud.

• Market participants must disclose project funding, emissions reduction methodologies, and credit retirements.

3. Stronger Oversight and Governance

• Regulatory agencies must actively monitor carbon trading to prevent market abuses.

• Establishing independent oversight bodies, similar to financial market regulators, will ensure integrity.

4. Strengthening Verification and Auditing

• Carbon offset projects must undergo independent third-party verification.

• Periodic audits and additionality enforcement are necessary to filter out low-quality credits.

5. Risk Management to Prevent Price Volatility

• Carbon price instability discourages long-term investment in emissions reduction projects.

• Policymakers can introduce:

• Price floors and ceilings to stabilize the market.

• Reserve mechanisms to adjust credit supply during price spikes.

• Minimum credit quality thresholds to ensure only high-integrity credits are traded.

Chapter 3: Unlocking Investment Pathways: Policy and Institutional Reforms for Scaled Climate Finance

Mobilizing finance at scale is essential to accelerating the global transition to a low-carbon economy. While green bonds and carbon markets provide effective mechanisms for directing capital toward climate solutions, a broader financial ecosystem must be developed to de-risk investments, align public and private sector financing, and enhance regulatory transparency. Governments, financial institutions, and multilateral organizations play a critical role in strengthening policy frameworks, expanding sustainable investment instruments, and ensuring climate-related financial risks are effectively managed.

This chapter explores key strategies for scaling climate finance, including enhancing financial regulations to integrate climate risks, aligning public and private sector investments, and implementing policy reforms to drive capital into sustainable infrastructure and low-carbon technologies. By developing clear taxonomies, robust disclosure frameworks, and investment incentives, policymakers can create a stable environment that fosters long-term, climate-aligned capital flows.

Strengthening Financial Frameworks for Green Investment

The transition to a low-carbon economy requires well-structured financial frameworks to mobilize investment at the scale necessary to meet global climate goals. Central banks, financial regulators, and multilateral institutions play a key role in integrating climate risks into financial systems, expanding blended finance mechanisms, and ensuring financial stability. Strengthening these frameworks is crucial for scaling green investments, particularly in emerging markets, where climate finance is most needed.

The Role of Central Banks, Financial Regulators, and Multilateral Institutions

Climate-related risks pose a systemic threat to financial stability, increasing the potential for stranded assets, credit defaults, and economic disruptions. As a result, financial institutions are integrating climate risk assessments to guide investments toward low-carbon, climate-resilient projects.

• **Central Banks**: Some central banks incorporate climate considerations into monetary policy and financial supervision. The Network for Greening the Financial System (NGFS) is promoting climate risk disclosure and green lending practices among global financial institutions.

• **Financial Regulators**: Regulators are introducing mandatory sustainability disclosures, ensuring investors have clear, reliable information on climate risks. The Task Force on Climate-related Financial Disclosures (TCFD) is helping standardize climate risk reporting, improving transparency.

• **Multilateral Institutions**: Development banks and organizations like the World Bank and IMF provide concessional funding, technical assistance, and policy guidance to promote sustainable investment strategies. They also play a role in mobilizing private capital through risk-sharing mechanisms and co-financing initiatives.

Integrating Climate Risks into Financial Stability and Regulations

Climate-related financial risks, including extreme weather events, resource scarcity, and carbon-intensive asset devaluation, can have systemic impacts on global financial markets. Macroprudential regulations help mitigate these risks by requiring financial institutions to assess and disclose climate-related risks.

• **Climate Stress Testing**: Many regulators are conducting climate stress tests to evaluate how financial institutions would perform under different climate scenarios. These tests help identify vulnerabilities and inform risk management strategies.

• **Capital Reserve Requirements for Green Investments**: Adjusted capital requirements incentivize sustainable lending. By assigning lower risk weights to climate-friendly loans, regulators encourage banks to finance green projects.

• **Green Asset Taxonomies**: **Standardized classifications** for sustainable investments help prevent greenwashing. The EU Taxonomy for Sustainable Activities is a leading framework that defines eligible green investments.

Expanding Blended Finance to Attract Private Capital in Emerging Markets

Emerging economies face high investment risks, making it difficult to attract private capital for sustainable projects. Blended finance, which combines public, philanthropic, and private funding, helps address this challenge.

• **Public-Private Co-Financing Models**: Governments and development banks can provide first-loss capital or loan guarantees to reduce financial risk for private investors. This encourages investment in sustainable infrastructure.

• **Green Credit Guarantees**: Financial institutions can issue green credit guarantees to protect against loan defaults for climate-related projects, supporting sectors such as renewable energy and sustainable agriculture.

• **Climate-Focused Investment Funds**: Institutions like the Green Climate Fund (GCF) and Global Environment Facility (GEF) use blended finance to mobilize private capital for large-scale low-carbon development projects.

Aligning Public and Private Sector Investments

Achieving global climate goals requires strong coordination between the public and private sectors to mobilize investment at scale. Governments create a stable investment environment through policies and regulations, while the private sector provides capital and innovation for sustainable growth. However, aligning these sectors requires strategic policies, financial incentives, and risk-reduction mechanisms to ensure that investment flows support climate objectives.

Public-Sector Leadership in Creating a Stable Investment Environment

Governments play a foundational role in directing private capital toward sustainable initiatives by establishing clear policies, financial incentives, and long-term regulatory stability.

• **Long-Term Policy Commitments**: Legally binding net-zero targets, carbon pricing mechanisms, and climate action roadmaps provide certainty for investors, encouraging long-term capital allocation to clean energy, low-carbon technologies, and climate-resilient infrastructure.

• **Regulatory Stability**: Consistent climate-focused regulations ensure that sustainable investments remain profitable and viable over time, preventing investor uncertainty caused by changing policies.

• **Public Investments as Catalysts**: Government investments in renewable energy, public transportation, and resilient urban infrastructure serve as benchmarks for private-sector engagement.

Strong public-sector commitment enhances investor confidence, unlocking greater private capital flows toward climate-aligned investments.

De-Risking Private Capital Through Public Guarantees and Concessional Finance

One of the biggest barriers to scaling climate finance is investment risk, particularly in emerging markets. Governments and development finance institutions can mitigate these risks through public guarantees, concessional finance, and risk-sharing mechanisms.

• **Public Guarantees**: Governments and development banks issue guarantees to protect investors from potential financial losses in climate projects, making sustainable investments more attractive.

• **Concessional Finance**: Institutions like the GCF and GEF provide low-interest loans, grants, and subsidies to climate projects, particularly in sectors with high upfront costs.

• **Risk-Sharing Mechanisms**: Public-private investment platforms, where development banks take on first-loss positions, reduce risk for private investors, encouraging participation in high-impact projects such as renewable energy expansion and sustainable agriculture.

By reducing financial risks, public-sector support mechanisms mobilize private capital, accelerating the transition to a low-carbon economy.

Corporate Net-Zero Commitments and ESG Disclosure Frameworks

Corporate commitments to net-zero emissions and ESG disclosure frameworks are transforming financial strategies, aligning private investment with climate goals.

• **Corporate Net-Zero Targets**: Many companies are committing to net-zero emissions by 2050, requiring significant investments in renewable energy, supply chain decarbonization, and carbon offsets. These commitments send strong market signals, attracting green finance.

• **ESG Disclosure Requirements**: Investors increasingly demand climate risk transparency. TCFD and Sustainability Accounting Standards Board (SASB) frameworks guide companies in reporting climate-related financial risks.

• **Green Financing Instruments**: Companies that meet sustainability performance targets gain access to sustainability-linked loans and green bonds, which offer preferential interest rates based on achieving climate objectives.

Policy Recommendations for Scaling Climate Finance

To achieve global climate targets and accelerate the transition to a low-carbon economy, scaling climate finance requires clear policy frameworks, standardized taxonomies, and targeted financial mechanisms. Governments, financial institutions, and regulatory bodies must collaborate to enhance transparency, expand green financing tools, and align institutional investments with climate goals. This section outlines key recommendations in three priority areas: developing global green finance taxonomies, expanding sovereign green bonds and national carbon markets, and strengthening climate-aligned investment mandates.

Developing Global Standards for Green Finance Taxonomies

A key challenge in climate finance is the lack of consistent definitions for green investments. Without harmonized taxonomies, investors struggle to assess whether financial products genuinely support sustainability goals, leading to greenwashing risks and inefficiencies. Establishing globally recognized green finance taxonomies enhances market credibility and transparency.

• The EU Sustainable Finance Taxonomy serves as a model, providing clear definitions of green activities and guiding sustainable investment.

• Global harmonization efforts should align taxonomies across Europe, North America, Asia, and developing markets to facilitate cross-border sustainable investments.

• Regulators should require financial institutions to disclose climate-related risks and ensure investment alignment with standardized taxonomies.

• Technology-driven verification systems (e.g., blockchain-based sustainability tracking) can improve reporting accuracy and prevent misclassification.

Establishing internationally recognized taxonomies creates a transparent, efficient, and trustworthy climate finance ecosystem.

Expanding Sovereign Green Bonds and National Carbon Markets

Sovereign green bonds and carbon pricing mechanisms play a critical role in financing climate action and attracting institutional investors. Expanding these tools at national and international levels will mobilize large-scale capital for sustainable development.

Sovereign Green Bonds

• Governments can issue sovereign green bonds to fund climate mitigation and adaptation projects, such as renewable energy, sustainable transport, and reforestation.

• Expanding sovereign green bond markets provides benchmarks for corporate issuances, improving market liquidity.

• Establishing transparent reporting and impact assessment frameworks ensures that green bond proceeds align with sustainability objectives.

National Carbon Markets

• Expanding carbon pricing mechanisms—including cap-and-trade systems and carbon taxes—creates economic incentives for businesses to reduce emissions while generating revenue for climate projects.

• Cross-border cooperation on carbon markets, such as linking the EU Emissions Trading System (EU ETS) with other national markets, enhances market efficiency.

• Governments can allocate carbon revenues to sovereign climate funds to finance green infrastructure and emissions reduction technologies.

By leveraging sovereign green bonds and national carbon markets, governments can mobilize large-scale finance, set benchmarks for private sector participation, and strengthen climate commitments.

Strengthening Climate-Aligned Investment Mandates for Institutional Investors

Institutional investors, including pension funds, insurance companies, and sovereign wealth funds, manage trillions of dollars in assets, making them key players in financing the low-carbon transition. Strengthening climate-aligned investment mandates ensures that capital flows toward sustainable projects.

Mandatory Climate Risk Disclosure

• Regulators should require institutional investors to disclose their exposure to climate risks under frameworks such as the TCFD.

• Transparency in investment strategies ensures that portfolios align with net-zero targets.

Fiduciary Duty Reforms

• Climate risk should be integrated into fiduciary duty regulations, requiring investors to consider long-term environmental risks and opportunities.

• Pension funds and insurers should prioritize climate-positive investments such as renewable energy, sustainable agriculture, and green infrastructure.

Incentivizing Green Investment Through Risk Mitigation

• Public finance institutions can offer co-investment opportunities, credit enhancements, and first-loss capital to attract institutional investors to emerging market sustainability projects.

• Blended finance models—combining public and private capital— can scale investments in low-carbon industries.

By aligning institutional capital with climate goals, pension funds, insurers, and sovereign wealth funds can play a transformational role in scaling sustainable finance and driving long-term economic resilience.

Conclusion

The expansion of green bonds and carbon markets represents a transformational shift in global finance, unlocking investment pathways for a net-zero future. However, realizing their full potential requires strong governance, regulatory clarity, and investor confidence.

Policymakers must prioritize the development of standardized green finance taxonomies, ensuring transparency and preventing greenwashing. Governments should scale sovereign green bond issuances and strengthen national carbon markets, sending clear signals to institutional investors. Expanding public-private partnerships and de-risking mechanisms will further accelerate private sector engagement in climate finance.

Financial institutions must integrate climate risk into investment strategies, aligning capital flows with sustainability goals. Institutional investors, including pension funds and sovereign wealth funds, must adopt climate-aligned investment mandates, mobilizing trillions in assets for sustainable growth.

The urgency of the climate crisis demands immediate action. Without scaled-up climate finance, achieving global net-zero targets will remain out of reach. Governments, businesses, and investors must act now—implementing ambitious reforms, strengthening green finance regulations, and ensuring that every dollar invested supports a sustainable, low-carbon future.

www.ingramcontent.com/pod-product-compliance
Lightning Source LLC
Chambersburg PA
CBHW060531280326
41933CB00014B/3133